POSITIVE MINDSET WORKBOOK FOR KIDS

How to Think Happy Thoughts, Stay
Motivated, and Overcome Challenges

About The Author

Psyd. Jane Artwood is a therapist and writer who has dedicated her life to helping others. With years of experience as a licensed therapist, she has helped countless individuals overcome a wide range of emotional and mental health challenges. She received her bachelor's degree in psychology from Columbia University and her master's degree in psychology from the University of Wisconsin. Driven by her passion for helping people, she has turned her attention to writing, using her expertise to create powerful tools and resources that can help even more people on their journey to better mental health. Her books are designed to provide practical and actionable advice, as well as support and encouragement, to anyone struggling with anxiety, stress, or other challenges. Other books from the author include:

This Book Belongs To

_____

TABLE OF CONTENTS

Introduction

Are you ready to unlock the power of a positive mindset? Get ready to dive into an enchanting journey with the Positive Mindset Workbook for Kids. This workbook is your secret potion to discovering the incredible magic that lies within you.

You'll engage in exciting games, artistic exercises, and intriguing prompts inside these pages that will assist you in developing a mentality that is full of sunshine, rainbows, and limitless possibilities. Together, let's investigate the amazing power of thankfulness, self-belief, and a whole lot more!

Imagine flying over the clouds of self-assurance, dousing the world with compassion, and sparking the flames of joy within you. You may channel your inner superhero while navigating difficulties and overcoming hurdles with the help of this workbook.

So, gather your courage, put on your adventurous spirit, and get ready to embark on a quest to uncover the secrets of a positive mindset.

CHAPTER 1

Unleashing Positive Mindset

What does it mean to have a positive mindset?

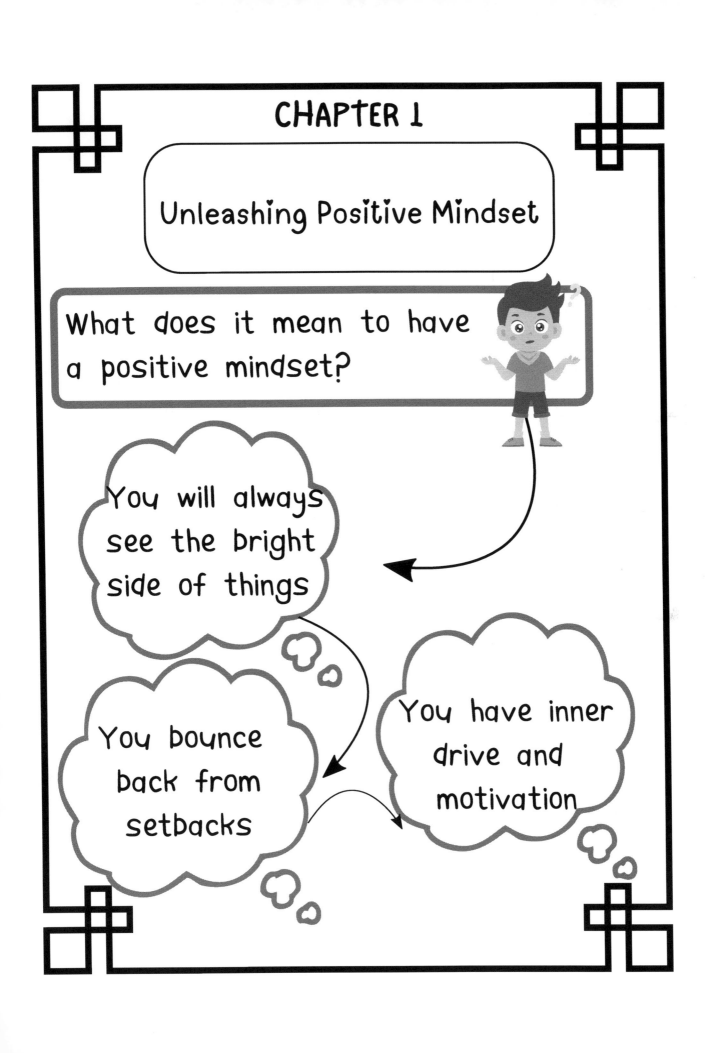

You will always see the bright side of things

You bounce back from setbacks

You have inner drive and motivation

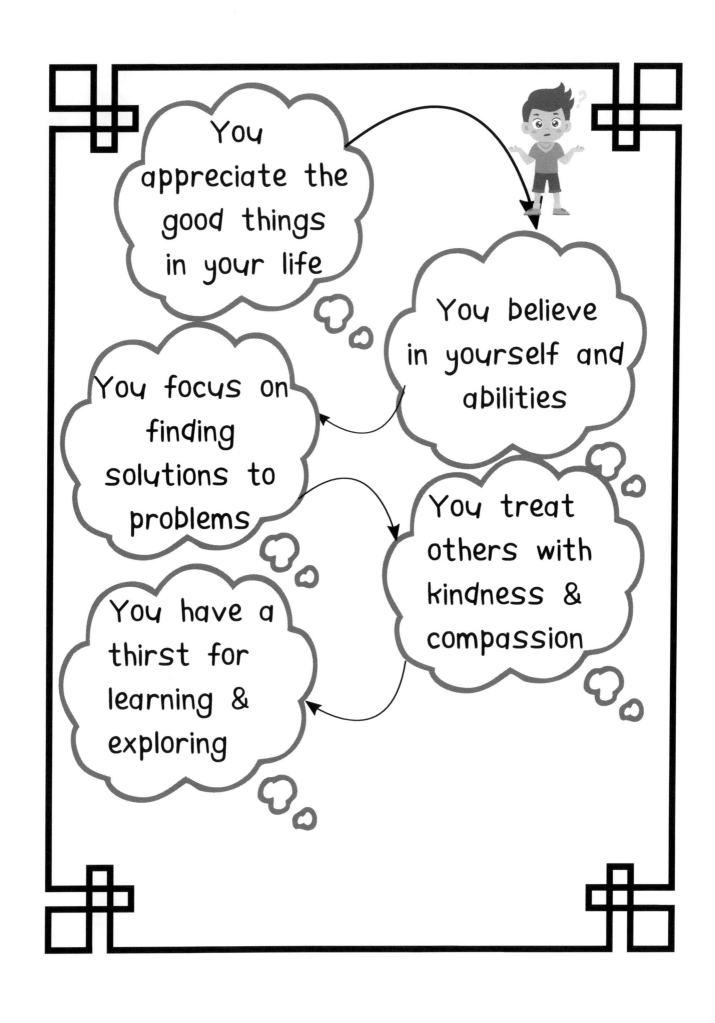

Activity:

Spend some time by yourself after carefully reviewing all the characteristics of a person with a positive mindset to see if you already have any of them.

The good news is that you will learn how to do it here if you don't already. Use the layout below to list the traits you already possess or would truly like to acquire.

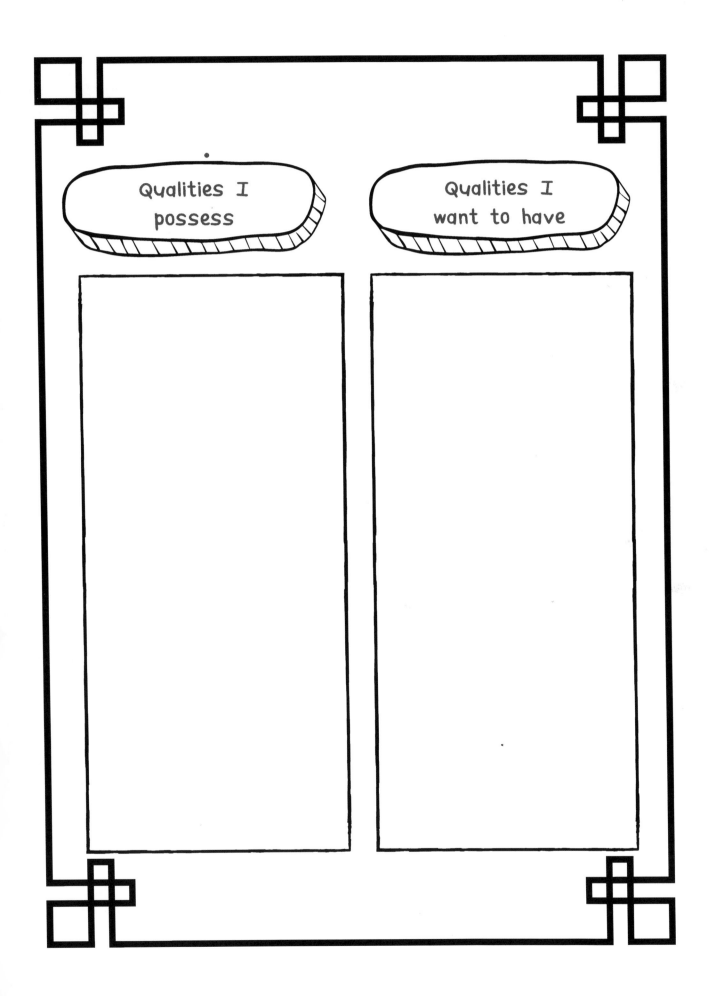

Qualities I possess

Qualities I want to have

How do you think having a positive outlook can impact your thoughts, feelings, and actions?

CHAPTER 2

Magic Mind Makeover

Ann was a girl who constantly had a cloud of unfavorable ideas hanging over her head. She would consistently have self-doubt and believe she wasn't good enough. She was depressed and discouraged from doing new activities as a result of these ideas.

Ann met a wise old bird one day who recognized her poor attitude. The bird explained to Ann the effectiveness of changing unfavorable ideas to favorable ones. Ann was intrigued and thought she'd try it.

Every time a negative thought popped into her mind, Ann would pause and challenge it. For example, when she thought, "I'll never be able to do it," she reminded herself, "I may not be able to do it now, but with practice and effort, I can improve."

Ann began gradually substituting positive affirmations for her negative ideas. Ann saw a tremendous improvement in her life as she changed her negative thinking.

She felt increasingly capable and self-assured as time went on. She realized she was capable of doing things she never imagined. She was no longer constrained by her self-defeating ideas, thus the world appeared brighter and more fascinating.

Activity:

I want you to learn how to transform negative ideas into good ones, just like Ann did. Take a step back, halt, and change any negative ideas into positive ones whenever you notice them.

I'll put down some unfavorable ideas and swap them out with good ones before letting you utilize your own expertise to finish the exercise. Good luck

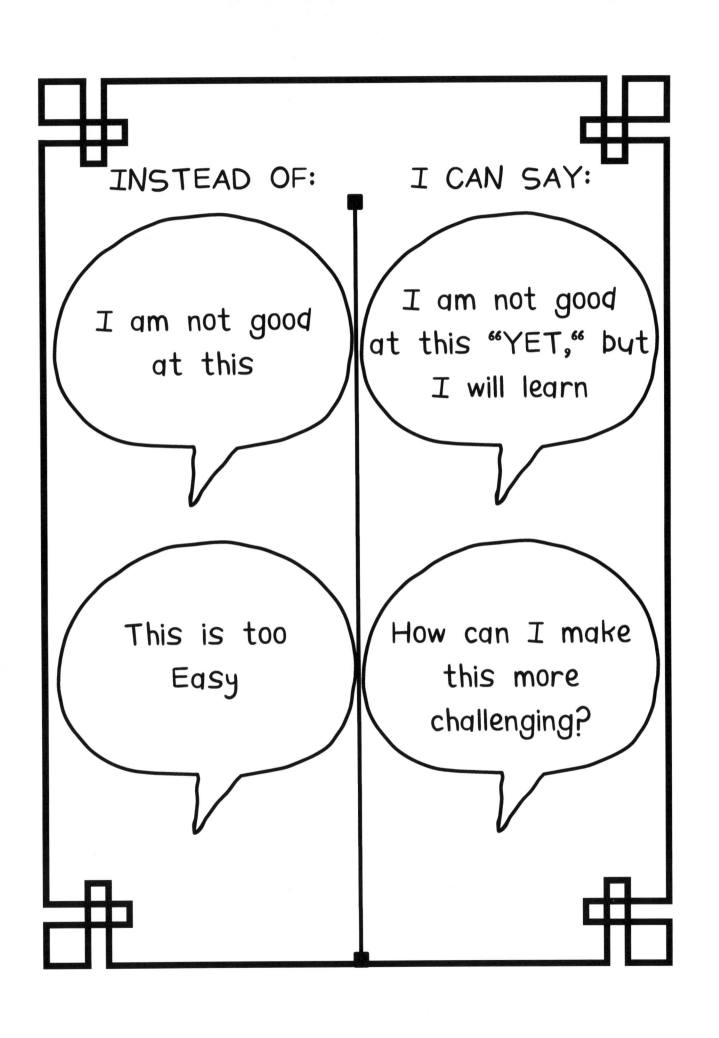

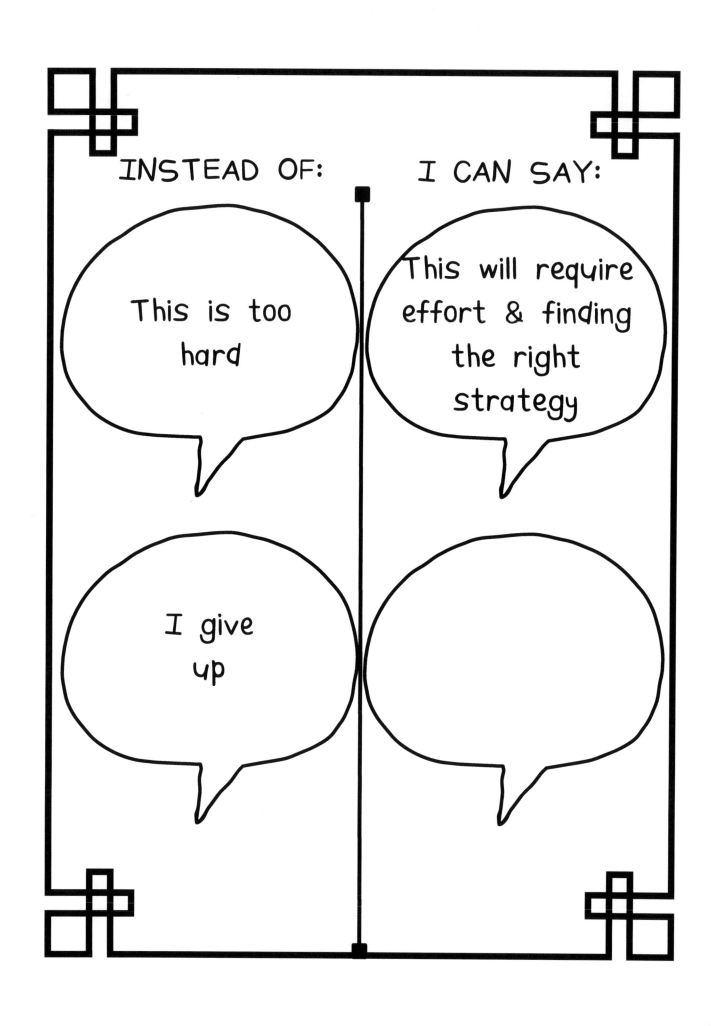

Write a list of something negative you always tell yourself and replace it with positive notes.

CHAPTER 3

Gratitude Harvesters

Being thankful and appreciative of the positive aspects of our lives-both significant and insignificant-is a key component in cultivating gratitude. It's similar to having a unique talent that enables us to see the bright side of things.

When we practice gratitude, we focus on what we have instead of what we don't have, which helps us feel happier and more content.

Having a positive mindset is like wearing a pair of magical glasses that make everything look brighter.

When we cultivate gratitude, it's like putting on those magical glasses because we start to notice all the good things around us.

Activity:

We'll start with a gratitude jar since they're a creative and enjoyable way to practice gratitude. In this exercise, you'll make a unique jar where you may store your daily expressions of gratitude.

Materials

- A clear jar (glass or plastic)
- Art supplies (ribbons, stickers, magazine cutouts, etc.)
- Gratitude slips (blank strips of paper, or slips with gratitude prompts)

Instructions

- Begin by personalizing your jar with decorations. Use ribbons, stickers, magazine cut-outs, items found in nature, or anything else you can imagine.
- After decorating the jar, it is time to add the first gratitude statements.

A gratitude statement acknowledges something that a person appreciates or is thankful for. Write it on your blank slips, for example:

- "I am grateful for waking up this morning"
- "I am thankful for my pet's health"
- "I appreciate the blue skies today."

Spend a brief period of time expressing the three expressions of thankfulness aloud to yourself after writing them down, one on each slip of paper. The thanks notes should then be folded and placed in the jar.

Complete the prompt below:

WHY I AM GRATEFUL

I am thankful for my family because..... _____

Something positive that occurred this week..... _____

I appreciate who I am because.......

WHY I AM GRATEFUL

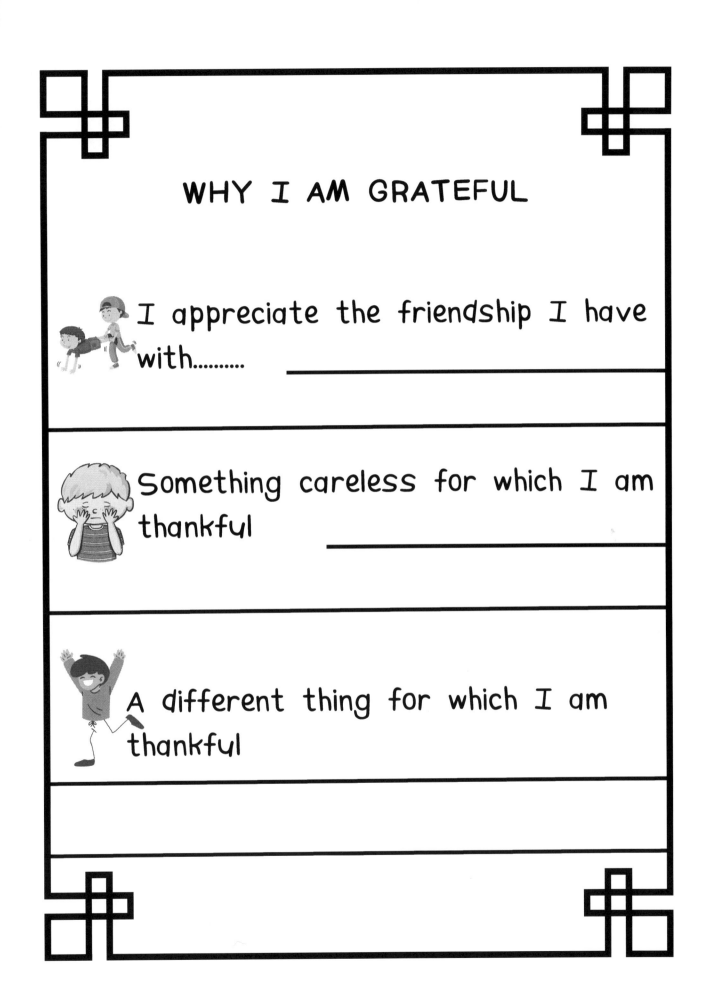

I appreciate the friendship I have with.......... _____

Something careless for which I am thankful _____

A different thing for which I am thankful

Complete the gratitude letter below to someone special in your life

To _____

Thank you for being my _____

I'm grateful to you because

1 _____

2 _____

3 _____

When I remember you, I feel.......

From: _____

How does gratitude make you feel?

What are you most grateful for and why?

CHAPTER 4

Championing Challenges

Imagine a world in which there were no obstacles to overcome and every day was the same. Although it would seem simple, it wouldn't be all that interesting, would it? Challenges provide excitement to life and help us develop into better versions of ourselves, just like puzzles or games do.

We get the possibility to learn new things and uncover our own inner power and capacity when we accept difficulties.

It resembles in-game leveling up! We may push ourselves to achieve things we never imagined we could by doing new things, learning about new things, and exploring new topics. Every obstacle we face helps us develop and gain self-confidence.

Activity:

Consider a skill you still need to acquire. You could wish to study more about a subject or issue that's challenging for you, take up a new pastime, or just hone your social skills.

Make a strategy for how you will learn it, and then go ahead and execute it. If your first attempt doesn't go as planned, you are always free to try again.

Smart Goals

Setting realistic and achievable outcomes.

My goal is:

S SPECIFIC

What do I want to happen?

M MEASURABLE

How will I know when I have achieved my goal?

A ATTAINABLE

Is the goal realistic and how will I accomplish it?

R RELEVANT

Why is my goal important to me?

T TIMELY

What is my deadline for this goal?

Smart Goals

Setting realistic and achievable outcomes.

My goal is:

S SPECIFIC

What do I want to happen?

M MEASURABLE

How will I know when I have achieved my goal?

A ATTAINABLE

Is the goal realistic and how will I accomplish it?

R RELEVANT

Why is my goal important to me?

T TIMELY

What is my deadline for this goal?

Smart Goals

Setting realistic and achievable outcomes.

My goal is:

S SPECIFIC

What do I want to happen?

M MEASURABLE

How will I know when I have achieved my goal?

A ATTAINABLE

Is the goal realistic and how will I accomplish it?

R RELEVANT

Why is my goal important to me?

T TIMELY

What is my deadline for this goal?

While having goals is crucial, we must also keep in mind that there are many other factors that are out of our control.

You must be aware of the difficulties you pursue. I'll include potential factors in the circle below that are under your control inside the circle and factors that are outside of your control outside the circle.

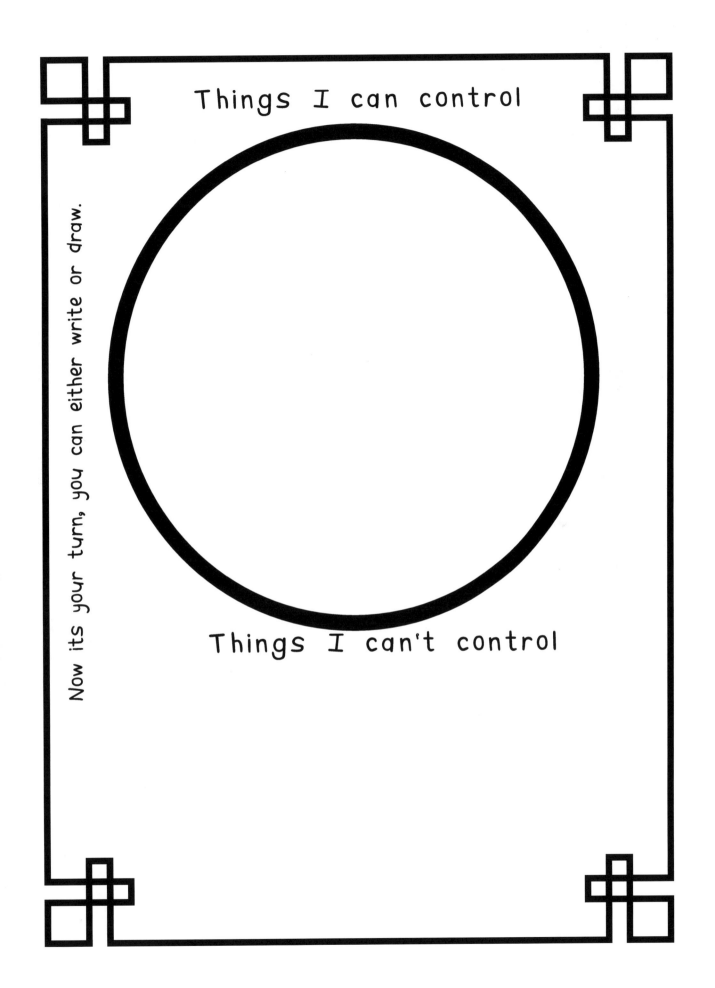

Things I can control

Things I can't control

Now its your turn, you can either write or draw.

Share a time when you faced a difficult
challenge. What was it, and how did you
feel?

Describe the steps you took to
overcome that challenge. How did you
stay motivated?

CHAPTER 5

Believe in You

Although Sharon was an intelligent and artistic girl, she frequently had self-doubt and was uncertain of her talents. She would contrast herself with others and worry that her skills or abilities weren't as strong.

One day, Sharon's teacher gave the students a new activity. Each student was required to compile a list of their accomplishments and strong points.

At first, Sharon was confused about what to write. But after receiving support from her teacher, she began to record her successes.

When Sharon considered her accomplishments, she saw that she had a lot to be proud of. She had participated in a school play, earned accolades for her artwork, and even assisted a friend with their math homework. These little successes started to give her more confidence.

After discovering her abilities and accomplishments, Sharon began to adopt a more optimistic outlook.

She came to understand that she was remarkable because of her unusual qualities and skills. She had stopped comparing herself to others since she was aware of the unique qualities she possessed.

Activity:

You must identify your qualities in this exercise, which might include leadership, kindness, intellect, creativity, and more. List everything out slowly and include others if you want, such;

- What my family considers to be my strong points

- What my teacher sees as my strongest points

- What my friends consider to be my strong points

CHARACTER STRENGTHS *shield*

Complete the shield as a whole class exercise,
then reflect on your own character strengths:

What I think are
my strengths

What my teacher
thinks are my
strengths

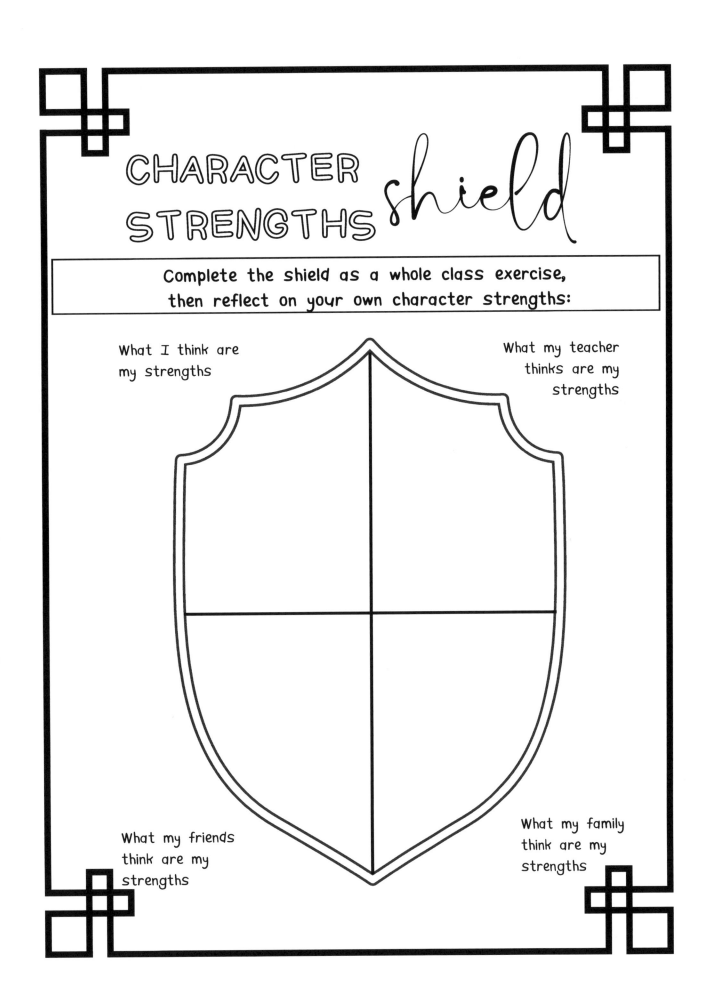

What my friends
think are my
strengths

What my family
think are my
strengths

Which of your many strengths do think is the strongest and why?

Which of your many strengths do think is the weakest and how can you improve on it?

CHAPTER 6

Positive Words

Using positive self-talk is like having an inner cheerleader! You feel better and more confident when you speak kindly and positively to yourself. Positive self-talk serves as a reminder of your talents and skills.

It enables you to have confidence in yourself and approach difficulties with a cheerful outlook.

Therefore, try replacing your negative ideas with positive ones the next time you see yourself doing so to observe how it improves your mood and makes you feel amazing. Positive self-talk makes you shine even brighter because you are awesome!

Some common ways to stop negative self-talk include:

Challenge core beliefs

Stop the thoughts

Let go perfectionism

Switch to positive self-talk

Activity:

How you talk to yourself is important. We are going to focus on positive self talk. On each petal, write something you like about yourself or something you are good at.

How do you feel when you speak
negatively to yourself?

How do you feel when you speak
positively to yourself?

CHAPTER 7

Rise and Shine

Learning to recover from hardships and maintain a positive outlook is a key component in developing resilience. It's like having the strength to resist powerful winds. When we are resilient, we don't allow difficulties to get the better of us. Instead, we work to get beyond them and keep moving forward.

Positivity is comparable to having a superpower. Even when things are difficult, it enables us to see the positive in any circumstance.

Resilience is a skill that may help us become stronger, braver, and more self-assured. We develop the ability to persist in our efforts and have faith in ourselves.

We can overcome any obstacle and emerge even stronger on the other side if we have resilience and a good outlook.

Activity:

I will create some common scenarios you may face daily, all you have to do is describe how you will handle such a difficult situation if you are truly resilient.

Your parents yell at you for not cleaning your room, what will you do?

_____

_____

_____

You feel as if no one likes you at school, what will you do?

You trip and fall in front of the whole school, what will you do?

Becoming resilient as a kid is an exciting journey! Here are some steps to help you cultivate resilience:

- Believe in yourself
- Stay positive
- Practice self-care
- Seek support
- Learn from setbacks

Reflect on a challenging situation you faced. How did resilience and a positive mindset help you navigate and overcome the difficulties?

Scoring yourself from 1-10, what would you score yourself when it comes to resilience and why?

CHAPTER 8

Positive Vibes Zone

Having supportive individuals around you lifts and inspires you, whether they be your parents, siblings, teachers, or close friends. They support you through both good and bad times, have faith in your ability, and encourage you.

Their optimism spreads to you and encourages you to look on the bright side of things.

Positive influences can motivate you to establish ambitious objectives and have self-confidence. They inspire you to follow your interests and ambitions and serve as a constant reminder that you are capable of great things.

They support your personal development by acknowledging your accomplishments and assisting you in learning from your errors.

Activity:

It is crucial to surround ourselves with people who make our days better. It is your obligation to enter their names in the space provided below and to constantly remind yourself that you may contact them if you feel like your thoughts are becoming negative.

You should constantly try to brighten their day and make sure they are folks you feel comfortable sharing with. Giving is more wonderful than receiving.

THE SUPPORT CIRCLE

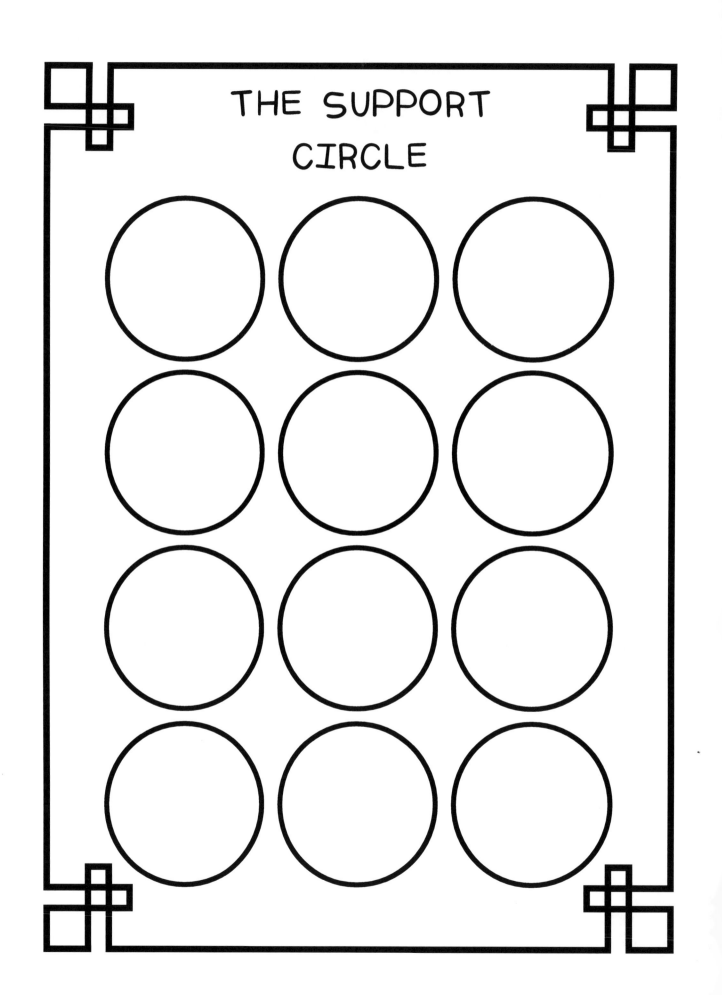

For those written in your support circle, How do they contribute to your well-being and help you maintain a positive mindset?

How can you strengthen your relationships with them?

CHAPTER 9

Celebrating Growth & Progress

Recognizing and celebrating personal growth and achievements is important because it makes us feel proud and happy about what we have accomplished. It shows us that we are making progress and getting better at things.

Celebrating our successes keeps us inspired and self-assured. It serves as a reminder that we are capable of achieving great things and overcoming obstacles.

We feel happier and more optimistic when we celebrate our development since it increases our self-confidence. Therefore, it's crucial to recognize our progress and the incredible things we are capable of.

Activity: Congratulations on making it this far in the workbook; you have accomplished a lot by reaching this chapter thus far, and I hope you have successfully navigated the many activities in earlier chapters.

It takes a lifetime to develop an optimistic outlook because we must constantly remind ourselves that things get better. You are to decorate the trophy, which is shown below, with your success. Every success, even if it is as simple as "I smile more frequently now" or "My self-care has improved," is to be commended.

How does recognizing your growth and progress contribute to your overall happiness and well-being?

Which accomplishment are you most proud of?

CHAPTER 10

Lifetime of Positivity

It's crucial to create a personal mantra-a brief statement that embodies a positive attitude-because it may help mold our ideas and beliefs. A mantra we repeat to ourselves repeatedly serves as a beacon for positivity and self-confidence, reminding us to stay that way.

It's similar to having a hidden ability that increases our self-confidence and enables us to go over obstacles. We may teach our brains to concentrate on the positive, have confidence in our skills, and approach life with optimism and resilience by developing a personal mantra.

It's as if we have our own personal magic phrase that, when spoken, gives us a boost of confidence and enables us to face any challenge.

Activity:

Choose the affirmation that resonates with you the most and repeat it to yourself regularly. Be reminded that these positive phrases can help shape your mindset and empower you to face life with optimism and resilience.

Remember you are allowed to add yours in the empty spaces below, think of something that can directly have a positive impact on your mindset.

Positive Mindset

Positive Mindset mantra. Add yours

Example: "I am capable of great things."

"I choose to think positive thoughts."

"I am unique and special just the way I am"

"I choose happiness and positivity every day."

"I have a bright and positive future ahead."

How do you feel saying this mantra to yourself daily?

Which activities did you enjoy the most in this workbook and why?

Made in the USA
Las Vegas, NV
05 January 2024

83859283R00044